CHATTAHOOCHEE CATS

CHATTAHOOCHEE CATS

Jenny Guberman

Jenny Guberman

**BOLD
STORY
PRESS**

Washington, DC

Bold Story Press, Washington, DC 20016
www.boldstorypress.com

First edition published December 2021

Library of Congress Control Number: 2021910120

ISBN: 978-1-954805-08-8 (paperback)
ISBN: 978-1-954805-09-5 (e-book)

Text and cover design by Laurie Entringer
Cover art and illustrations by Susan Mitchell

Printed in the United States of America
10 9 8 7 6 5 4 3 2 1

For Gemma and Luke
and animal lovers and rescuers everywhere

Contents

Prologue

Meriwether and Camille live with their mother, Pearl, a brother, and two sisters in a quiet town by the sea. Their father lives nearby in a log. The seven cats have a good life, but it hasn't always been that way for Pearl. Last year, a kind person named Sam found Pearl lost in the Florida Everglades. He invited her to live with him.

Before then, Pearl had never thought about being a mother. She also didn't imagine that when she met a handsome black and white neighborhood cat, they would soon announce their wedding. They invited many cats and, of course, Sam. The happy couple was given catnip treats as they left for their seaside honeymoon.

Soon, Pearl looked proudly over a basket of five kittens: three black with white bibs and paws, and two entirely black. Once they could walk, the kittens tumbled out of their basket and marched out the door to explore the world.

Each morning, they greet their father sitting on his log. All day long, they climb up a coconut tree or dash under a bush, hunting a chipmunk or lizard. In the evening, they chase fireflies in the garden and watch their father while he hunts mice until their mother calls them indoors.

It's fun to play outside, but the kittens also like playing indoors. They find endless joy in swinging on the living room curtains, jumping on the kitchen cabinets, diving into the laundry basket, or chasing their tails. When they are tired, they sleep in a heap on a sunny windowsill.

Although she likes their bold spirit, Pearl reminds her kittens to always obey her. Otherwise, they won't be allowed to play on their own. In her early life as a stray, she rarely had a good meal. She doesn't want her kittens to get lost and have the same thing happen to them, so she keeps an eye on them.

Once they are eight weeks old, three of the kittens leave to live with families that have adopted them. At first, Pearl, Meriwether, and Camille miss them a lot. Pearl licks their tiny faces to comfort them and hugs them warmly. She tells them that their brother and sisters are very loved, and they will be happy. Secretly, she is glad that at least Camille and Meriwether are staying with her. She knows that together, the three of them will have many adventures.

1 THE BIG ROAD TRIP

It's May when Sam, their big person, places cat carriers on the living room floor. Surprised, they sniff and circle the carriers, but they don't see anything inside. Sam picks the kittens up and places them in one of the carriers. He puts their mother, Pearl, inside the other one.

"Mother, where are we going?!" meow Meriwether and Camille.

"To the Chattahoochee!" she replies.

"The Chattahoochee?" Camille repeats. "Well, I guess that's all right. As long as we're not going to the vet for shots."

Meriwether is too busy playing with a toy mouse to comment.

As the car pulls out of the driveway, Pearl reminds them, "Don't forget to say goodbye to your father!" There he sits on his stump in the morning sunlight. He decided to stay behind to control the mouse population in the Everglades and to continue his carefree life. With a wave of a white paw and a swish of his handsome tail, he gives them all a fond goodbye.

"We'll miss you, Dad," cry the kittens, waving. With that, they are off.

"Woohoo!" chirp the excited cats as the silver sedan drives onto the highway. They are ready to see the wonders of the world. They can't wait to see that distant place: the Chattahoochee!

Pearl likes riding in cars, and so do her kittens. Squinting through the windows, they see many sights: sunny skies, coconut trees, colorful birds, canals, and drawbridges. Later, lakes and rivers appear, and trees with clouds of gray-green Spanish moss dripping from their branches. Then horses and cows grazing in lush pastures dot the countryside on both sides of the road.

Suddenly, Camille raises her voice, "What are these strange white birds?"

"They are ibises, and they live all over southern Florida in the wetlands," says Sam.

Finally, around five p.m., after passing miles of billboards, they are blinded by the sight of a gold-topped building. Seeing the kittens blink in surprise, Pearl laughs. "It's not your imagination; that's the capital of Georgia! Welcome to Atlanta!"

At last, after hours of sitting in their carriers behaving themselves, the three cats have arrived at their destination: Atlanta! The city's grand skyline spreads out before them. They can see skyscrapers, busy streets, sports stadiums, museums, the Georgia Aquarium, Centennial Park with its Fountain of Rings, a sky wheel, and the proud Olympic torch.

Tucked behind a saucer magnolia tree on a quiet street is a peach-colored cottage. Standing guard in the backyard are two giant water oaks. The kittens jump out of the car and run around, happily exploring their new surroundings. In the distance, they can see the Chatta-hoochee River glittering in the afternoon sun.

"Mom!" the kittens shout while chasing a squirrel. "Is this our new home?"

"Keep looking," Pearl replies as she crept among the camellias.

Meriwether calls out at the furthest point of the yard, "Look over here, Camille!"

A handsome green barn with a pretty sign in white letters says Meriwether Mews. "Wow! It's named after me!" Meriwether smiles.

Camille turns to a lovely path that winds through a cluster of flowers to the top of the hill. "Meriwether! Mom! Come see this!" Fluttering in the breeze, a color-ful banner spells Camille's Canter.

"This is the way!" Camille shouts. Winding up the hill, they follow the path through the trees until it ends at an open gate. The three cats go through it into an arena surrounding the barn. Two huge doors and two small-er doors with flaps introduce them to the barn. What a great discovery! A window box with dancing flowers welcomes them. "Glad you're here!" it seems to say.

Once inside the barn, they spy a ladder reaching to a loft with two windows. This is a whole new world—one where they feel both safe and free to roam. Pearl smiles. "Can you tell, my dears? We're home!"

High up in the loft, the three cats sink into three soft beds, tired from their long journey. Sleepily, through the windows, they watch squirrels and chipmunks run in the tree branches. Multicolor birds swoop around a bird feeder. In the distance, they spy silver fish rising from the Chattahoochee.

The happy kittens decide to write a story about their new home. "Mom, will you help us?" they meow.

"Why, of course!" Pearl nods as they drift off into a well-earned slumber.

A gentle breeze brushes each one, whispering, "The Chattahoochee awaits."

2 Shooting the Hooch

Before sunrise, Meriwether opens one eye, then the other one. He glances over at his sister and pokes her. "Wake up, Camille!" The birds are already singing. The squirrels scamper in the branches of the trees outside the window. "Let's climb the oak tree before Mom wakes up."

Silently, they creep through the door flap to look at the two giant oaks. "Do you really want to do this?" Camille looks at the trees nervously.

"It's easy," Meriwether calls down to his sister from three limbs up. "Just put one paw in front of the other, count to four, and repeat."

Before she knows it, Camille is six limbs ahead of her brother. "I love this!" she shouts. "Race you to the top!"

There is a wonderful view at the top of the giant tree. All around them is a hive of activity. There are baby birds in nests cheeping for worms, squirrels chattering to one another, and an owl sitting in a hole in the trunk.

"This is all well and fine, Meriwether, but now, how do we get down?" Camille asks.

"Watch the squirrels," he suggests. Just then, one zips by, swinging like it's on a trapeze.

Carefully, Camille swings to a lower branch. "Not too bad! Come on, Meriwether!" It feels like flying as they jump down the branches until they reach the ground. "High fives," they say. "Mom will be proud!"

"You kittens are doing well," Pearl says as they groom themselves later. The day before, she asked Sam to take them on a trip to the Chattahoochee. It was time for the kittens to see the river up close, she said, and she wanted to share her love of water.

"What a good idea and a great way to beat the heat,"

Sam agreed, stroking his red beard.

After breakfast, he puts the cats safely in their carriers. With the windows rolled down and the wind in their fur, they drive toward the river.

During the ride, Pearl tells them stories of her dog-paddling days in Florida. "I surfed at the shore and made my friends laugh by sliding down riverbanks on my tummy," she brags. "In fact," she winks at Sam, "didn't I look more like an otter than a cat?"

"You were a perfect seal!" he replies, his blue-green eyes twinkling.

Following a yummy lunch of tuna melts, Sam lies down for a nap under a willow tree. Down to the water's edge walk the cats. The closer they get to the river, the muddier their paws become. Meriwether hears something croak. "What's that?" he yells.

"It's only a frog," says his mother, "and they're hard to catch because of their slippery skin."

One muddy paw after another, Meriwether walks in until all four paws are in the babbling river. He calls to his sister, "Catch up, Camille, this mud feels great!"

"Meow," she complains, up to her elbows in the sticky stuff.

"Be careful, you two!" says their mother as she wades deeper into the Chattahoochee, all four paws moving together.

"We're coming," say the kittens bravely as they slip in over their heads, their small legs paddling. With all three noses poking above the water, the cats can easily be mistaken for a family of beavers. They splash and chase minnows, enjoying the water wonderland.

"Stay near the shore!" warns their mother.

Her words are too late. The river's fast current takes the kittens away from their mother. It pulls them toward the rapids. Scared, they try to swim and cry for help, but it doesn't work.

Pearl knows that alone she cannot save them. She turns and swims back to shore, where Sam is still napping. He can save them!

At the same time, a river keeper walks near the water, looking for boaters who are not wearing their life jackets. As soon as he sees the scared kittens trying to swim out of danger, he runs to help. He picks up a long tree limb lying on the ground, then runs ahead. As the poor kittens are swept around the bend toward him, he throws the branch into the rapids. "Take it," he yells. "I'll pull you to shore!"

Using all their strength, the kittens catch the branch and hold onto its rough bark. The river keeper slowly pulls them out of the river.

Because of the river keeper's fast thinking and the kittens' bravery, everyone is safe. Shaking and coughing, Meriwether and Camille dry themselves off. Pearl and Sam thank the river keeper for being a hero.

"How can we show our thanks?" they ask him.

"All I want is your promise never to swim in the rapids again without wearing life jackets," he answers.

Pearl and Sam gently scold the kittens in the car as they go home. Very tired, they climb the ladder to the loft. They are surprised to see a large plate of salmon waiting next to their water bowl. Never too tired for salmon, they eat the food. They feel grateful to Sam for the yummy treat, even though he slept through them almost getting swept away on the river. As they fall asleep, they try to remember if they saw any salmon swimming in the Chattahoochee.

3 A Strange Sight

After their adventure on the river, the kittens look out the window. It is a fresh June day. A nice walk around the block is on their minds. They want to go before all the joggers and dog walkers come out.

Pearl warns them with a shake of her paw, "Stay out of trouble!"

When they trot out the gate, the sky is pink and purple from the sunrise. Last night's rain has left puddles and leaves all over the sidewalk. Splashing up the street, the two river-wise kittens see that they are not alone. Coming toward them is a young black cat with big orange eyes. It stops, trips, then stops again. The poor cat, wearing a collar and a leash, is trying to walk in a straight line. But it can't focus while exploring and jumping in the puddles. It trips right and left, forward and backward.

"That's a strange-looking cat," Camille says.

"Good morning," Meriwether says to the black cat. "Are you new in the neighborhood?"

The cat stops and stares. "I have lived here since I was a young sprout. In fact, my name is Sprout. And this is my big person, Adele."

Meriwether and Camille introduce themselves. They say that they also learned to walk with a leash. Now Sam trusts them to walk on their own.

The new big person smiles at the cats. "You can walk alone too one day, Sprout," Adele says. "After you learn about cars, dogs, and people. Let's invite your new friends over for a play date."

"Yay! When?" the cats shout.

"Saturday?" she says.

Sprout gives them his address. With a wave and a wobble, he walks up the sidewalk in his special way.

Adele cheers him on every step of the way. Excited, Meriwether and Camille skip around the block and jump in every puddle.

4 The Whistler

Saturday morning dawns warm and misty. As Meriwether and Camille walk to Sprout's house, a beautiful, strong whistle floats over the morning air.

The whistle turns into a whistler—the coolest character on a bike they have ever seen! He wears a bright orange and yellow vest and a winter hat. Earflaps hang down to his chin. It's Whistling Willie, a homeless person, pedaling by with Annie, his little brown and black dog by his side. Annie grew up in the country, but she has become very street smart since moving to Atlanta. She loves Whistling Willie and cats—as in CHASING THEM!

Uh oh! Meriwether and Camille waste no time. They climb into the first tree they see, with long branches that give instant safety.

Far from Annie, the kittens call down, "Hello, Whistling Willie!"

"Hello!" he replies. "We're on our way to the zoo." Every Saturday, Whistling Willie performs for the zoo crowds. They love his whistle and the beat of the bongo drummers. The drummers like to sit next to Whistling Willie on a low stone wall and perform without asking for money. Somehow, Whistling Willie and the drummers always leave at the end of the day with their pockets jingling.

"Where are you off to?" Whistling Willie asks, looking up at the kittens while Annie wags her tail below.

Trying to catch their breath, they reply, "We...we're trying to visit our new friend, Sprout, who lives across Boulevard."

"Boulevard, eh? That's a very busy street. Be sure to look both ways when you cross," he warns them.

"We will," they nod atop the tree.

"Have a beautiful day!"

As soon as Whistling Willie and Annie are out of sight and the whistles have faded, they climb down the tree.

They forget about Annie's barking to face the next challenge ahead. Sprout lives half a mile from the railroad tracks on the other side of Boulevard. Cars have to slow down as they reach the tracks, so the kittens cross Boulevard there. They take time to look both ways before running across the street in five giant leaps.

Safely across the road, their thoughts turn happily to Sprout and the treats they carry in their backpacks: salmon bites and a sprig of catnip from the garden.

5 Saved by a Bear

At the top of the steps on Sprout's porch, Camille stands on Meriwether's shoulders to reach the doorbell.

"Welcome to Sprout's house!" says Adele as she greets them. Sprout has a toy mouse in his mouth, which he drops at their paws. Off they all go, running around the house until Adele calls for a time out. "Snacks, catnip, and naps for the next thirty minutes," she orders.

"Thirty minutes is too long," all the kittens groan to each other.

"I have an idea," Meriwether says. "Do you have an attic?"

"Yes," Sprout replies, "but the only way up is by the

pull-down stairs."

Adele agrees to pull the stairs down after their nap. "However," she says, "The limit is forty-five minutes up there. I'll come look for you afterward."

"Awesome!" they shout as they munch on salmon bites.

When it's time for their trip to the attic, Camille pauses. "Uhm mm..." she says in a small voice, looking up at the dark, square hole in the ceiling. "I don't like cobwebs or spiders."

"Come on," Sprout says, excited. "There may even be bats. It's worth it!"

Camille replies "I do love bats. Alright, count me in."

The three kittens jump up the steps to the attic. They creep carefully along the old floorboards, then dart in between old suitcases, fans, boxes of dusty books, and holiday decorations.

"It's spooky up here," Camille says, still unsure if she wants to be there at all.

She gasps as Meriwether pounces on a lizard.

WHAM! Whether it was Meriwether's pounce or something else, the trap door slams shut.

"Oh no, oh, help! We're stuck!" cry the kittens. Their shouts, whimpers, and meows fade into silence; no one hears their small cries.

Far back in the dusty attic, the kittens spy a tiny ray of hope. A dim window in the afternoon sunlight promises a way out. Before they can check it out, something big, round, and brown crashes through the window. All three kittens run to hide behind a trunk.

"Is it a meteor?" Meriwether whispers.

"No, it has claws," Sprout says.

The hairy, round thing bursts into tears. Carefully walking toward it, Camille says, "Are you okay?"

Large bear tears roll down its furry cheeks. "No, I am not," sobs the bear cub. "I got lost trying to find my way back to the zoo. So I climbed a tree to look around. When I saw you playing inside the attic, I tapped on the window, but the branch I was standing on snapped, and I fell through it. Oh, please help me!" begs the cub.

"Don't worry. We'll help you," the kittens tell him.

"What's your name?"

"My name is Percy, short for Percival. I'm a Kodiak bear. My parents are from Alaska, but I was born in the zoo. I've never been anywhere else." He sobs some more.

The kittens introduce themselves. "If you can help us get out of the attic, we'll help you get back to the zoo," Meriwether says. "It's not far away. We'll show you the way home."

"I'll stay here in case Adele comes back," Sprout says.

With that, Percy, Camille, and Meriwether scramble out the window and climb down the tree trunk. Then the cub, with the two kittens on his back, runs across the railroad tracks, up two blocks on Boulevard, and through the zoo's entrance.

Meanwhile near the zoo, a huge search for Percy, the missing cub, finds few clues. A trail of small tracks ends at the sidewalk. There are police on horses with binoculars and dogs sniffing for a scent. Volunteers search the whole park for the cub. TV cameras film the scene. The bear habitat keeper stands scratching his head in confusion, wondering if this is all his fault. Percy's mother and father pace up and down, scared for their baby. What a mess!

Suddenly, like a miracle, a brown bear cub climbs into the tree outside the bears' home. Everyone watches in amazement as Percy drops into the den. The crowd cheers, the horses whinny, the dogs bark, the police honk their horns, the TV host cries, the zookeeper blows a thousand air kisses. But no one is happier than Percy to be safely back with his mom and dad.

Once everyone is calm again, the kittens go home. Adele apologizes to Sprout. She explains that she wanted to help find the lost cub, so she had asked her neighbor to check on the kittens while she went to the zoo. Her neighbor must have seen the stairs to the attic and put them back in place, not knowing the kittens were up there. "I am so sorry!" she says to Sprout. "Anyway, how was your play date?"

"We had a great time!" Sprout says, and he meant it.

Back at the green barn, Pearl eyes her kittens. "Did

you go to the zoo with Sprout today?" she asks slyly. "Percy, the Kodiak cub, escaped from the zoo. Luckily he found his way back. I saw it all on TV: a little brown bear racing across the park. Funny thing, I thought I saw two kittens riding on his back... Well, it's been a long day for everyone. Good night."

Meriwether and Camille smile and tumble into their beds.

6 Zippity Zoo Day

It's time we zipped over to the zoo for a visit," Pearl says. "Zoo Atlanta is only two blocks away. It's full of fur, fins, and feathers. We will even meet some relatives, like the Florida panther."

On the way over, Pearl talks about the alligators in Florida. "Wait until you see these creatures! Your father and I saw many of them lurking in the lakes, just waiting for a lost kitten or puppy. They'd stare at us with their beady eyes, and I knew they were thinking what tasty bites we would make."

Meriwether gulps. "I thought those were just logs in the water."

At the zoo's entrance, Camille jumps up and down. "Look at those tall birds with pink feathers! They're standing on one leg, and so are their chicks. Oh, poor things, they fall right over. Look, they are all white! When do the chicks turn pink?"

"When they're a few years old, my darlings," Pearl answers. "The color in the algae they eat turns them pink." Camille and Meriwether sit on a wall close to the flamingoes. They watch the birds snacking on the food they had stirred up from the bottom of the lake, hoping to see them turn pink.

A big sign says African Plains. The three cats head up the path to a habitat where they notice that the elephants inside look red, not gray. "It's the Georgia clay that changes their color when they bathe in the mud," Pearl explains.

Nearby, a mother giraffe and her baby munch leafy green branches fed to them by some children standing on a platform with a zookeeper. A zebra rubs its back against a tree. A camel basks in the sun. Meriwether shouts, "Totally awesome!"

"Rowrrrr!" All three cats jump, their tails bristling. They creep toward an exhibit where a lion roars from atop a giant rock. "It's feeding time for the African lions," says Pearl. "Let's move on quickly!"

At the Living Treehouse, Meriwether and his sister relax. They laugh as they watch the monkeys play. "Wow! They're like us the way they swing from limb to limb," Meriwether says.

"I do love tree climbing," Camille says. "Except when Annie is chasing us."

Next, they hop over to the marsupial exhibit. Kangaroos play hopscotch on a dusty patch of earth. Pearl watches them with their babies. "If only I had a pouch, I could keep you kittens out of trouble paws-free!"

Continuing up the path to the Amphibian and Reptile Experience, they stop for a drink of water. A sign pointing toward the Alaskan Kodiak Bears catches their eyes. "Wait, Mom, we have to see the bears!" Meriwether says.

At the bear enclosure, their friend Percy clambers over to the edge of the moat and stands on his hind legs, smiling and waving. The kittens wave back. "Isn't that the bear cub that escaped yesterday? He seems to know you." Pearl glances at her kittens.

"He sure looks like him," they reply, winking at each other. "What a friendly little cub! We must see him again soon!"

As they move up the ramp to the reptile exhibit, they see alligators basking on a sandbank. A hungry one rumbles. The cats walk past colorful habitats of snakes, toads, turtles, and lizards. They reach a huge tank where dolphins swim and dive with joy. "They're putting on a show for us!" the kittens cry.

As they are about to exit the pavilion, Meriwether spots a door marked "Staff Only—Do Not Enter." Curious, he watches an employee walk through with a bucket of fish. Not wasting the moment, he grabs his sister, and they dart through the open door.

Blinded by bright light, everything looks fuzzy. "What do you see, Camille?" Meriwether asks, blinking.

"I see the outline of something big, and it's breathing." Camille shivers. "I wish we were back with Mom."

Meriwether refuses to be scared. He remembers something he has seen. "It's a blimp!"

"A what?" Camille says.

"It's like the Goodyear blimp that floats above the stadium at football games," he replies, staring at the blimp. The stunning balloon is painted with lush trees, flashy birds, and slithering reptiles.

"What's it doing here?" Camille meows.

Staff wearing yellow Zoo Atlanta T-shirts scurry about loading empty cages, crates, and aquariums into the airship's hold. "I don't know," whispers Meriwether. "But let's find out."

"Okay, brave brother, I'm all for space travel," Camile replies. "But what does this blimp have to do with the zoo?"

Just then a zookeeper appears, busy getting ready for take-off. "Want to come along?" the zookeeper asks the kittens. "We are leaving on a trip to the Amazon Basin. Zoo Atlanta is allowed to bring back a few exotic species for education. You can help calm down any scared animals on the flight."

Happy to be part of such an important journey, the kittens agree to join.

7 Flying High

Walking up the ramp into the blimp, the kittens enter a vast cargo space. The moist and humid air re-creates the habitat of the rainforest. Meriwether and Camille sit in a row of seats and look around the inside of the blimp as one of the zoo attendants fastens their seatbelts. They watch as the ropes holding down the blimp are released.

"Welcome aboard and enjoy your flight. Buckle up and prepare for lift-off," the captain says. The kittens imagine the wonders of the rainforest as the noisy blimp rises into the sky.

Although it is warm inside the blimp, Camille decides to take her knitting out of her backpack to work on a winter mitten. A skilled knitter, she rarely pauses when she reaches the end of a row, so she lets her thoughts stray. Camille imagines meetings with jaguars, monkeys, macaws, and frogs. She already knows about red-eyed and poison dart frogs from seeing them at the zoo.

With her thoughts on the jungle, Camille jabs the canvas covering the side of the blimp by accident. She doesn't hear the hissing sound because it's so noisy inside the blimp. At the end of four rows, though, she sees that something is wrong. She tells Meriwether, relaxing beside her in an aisle seat, to get one of the zoo attendants.

Now stretched larger, the hole needs not one but three attendants to try to seal it with super glue. But the gap keeps growing as they fly higher, and they fail.

Hearing the dreadful news, the captain quickly calls Mission Control on the radio. "Mayday! Mayday!" he shouts.

"End the mission!" comes the response. "Focus on the safety of the passengers and crew."

The captain instructs everyone to strap on their parachutes and prepare to jump.

The passengers and crew stand nervously at the blimp's gaping hole. "Count to ten and jump," the captain commands. Camille can only count to eight, so Meriwether links paws with her, and they jump together. Once their parachutes unfold, they marvel as the rainforest spreads out below. It's like a rainbow of colors rising to greet them.

Soon, a rescue helicopter leaves Rio de Janeiro. It flies over the dense and steamy forest, searching for the blimp. It's not long before the pilot spots the blimp's crew huddling together on the banks of the Amazon. Tattered shreds of the blimp lay scattered nearby.

The helicopter lands in the closest open spot it can find. Everyone is found safe until a crewmember points to a clump of empty harnesses. "Where are the two kittens?" she cries. No kittens can be seen or heard. "Oh, no," she shouts. "The rainforest has swallowed them up!"

Although sad about the missing cats, the helicopter pilot says he will fly low and track them with his radar.

If he can't find them, the kittens will have to rely on their good instincts to find their way home before kitty school starts in the fall.

Alas, mist and trees cover the banks of the Amazon River. Any bare spots look muddy and bumpy. It's impossible to spot the two black and white kittens.

8 Amazon Rainbow

Meriwether and Camille hit the ground on all fours. They slowly untangle themselves from their parachutes. There is no sign of the blimp's crew, and they stand on a swampy, strange land. When they see the helicopter skimming over the jungle, they wave, but it flies on.

The sticky warmth of the jungle surrounds them. Macaws call to each other, the red-eyed tree frogs' voices croak in a contest with the harlequin and tiger frogs. A golden toad startles Camille as it ribbits.

The ground shifts under Camille's paws. "Meriwether! The ground is rising!" But that's not all.

"Gadzooks!" Meriwether shouts, also surprised.

"We're not standing on the ground; it's way too slimy and bumpy!"

What happens next defies all belief. The log the kittens stand on is alive! It's the back of an alligator, two times larger than any they had ever seen. The sight of the gator's eyes sends shivers up and down their tiny spines.

"Why did we ever want to see what was on the other side of that door at the zoo?" sobs Meriwether as they rise higher.

"If we die, Mom's really going to be sad," Camille wails. "We can't give up!"

But as the granddad of all alligators opens its jaws wide, revealing row upon row of sharp, glittering teeth, the kittens know the end was in sight. All they can do is hug each other.

"We're sorry, Mom," they shout into the air. "Please, can't you hear us and help us out of this mess? We promise we will never be naughty again. Please, Mom, send your magical cat spirit right now!"

In the wink of an eye—an alligator's eye—they catch a spark of hope. It's not the end after all! Here, in the Amazon, where nothing is ordinary, lives a fantastic alligator. To their surprise, those jaws do not chomp down on them. Those teeth do not crunch them like salmon bites. Instead, a perfect rainbow floats from the alligator's mouth. Speechless, they gape at the dazzling sight.

"I am not here to eat you up," the special alligator says kindly to them. "I'm here to rescue you and send you safely home to your mother. Many years ago, she found me in a Florida lake with my leg stuck in a steel trap. She told wildlife control, and they saved me. I was then flown to my birthplace in the Amazon, where I have lived happily ever since." At that, the alligator surrounds the kittens in the rainbow and beams them back to their green barn in Georgia.

Pearl's worst fears are over. Her old friend, Bumpy, has indeed returned the favor by sending her kittens home safe and sound.

"Mom," purr the happy kittens. "Cat's honor, we will never be disobedient again."

Pearl heaves a sigh. "Harrumph!"

9 Kitty School

Sam and Pearl had always homeschooled the kittens. The early months of their kittenhood were packed with learning and practicing skills such as climbing, stalking, pouncing, swimming, fishing, hissing, and catapult.

But at seven months of age, they are ready for kitty school, which begins at the end of August. Early in the morning of the first day, Pearl announces, "Rise and shine! Time for school!"

As if they don't know it! Sporting fresh haircuts, nail trims, and backpacks filled with notebooks, pencils, sardines, and water bowls, the two tuxedo kittens hug their mother. With proud steps, they trot down to the corner of Magnolia and Elm.

As the big yellow bus pulls up, Marmalade Mike opens its doors to welcome them. "We've got quite a clutter of kittens in here," he says. "Join the joy!"

Eagerly, they bound up the steps and find a seat next to Sprout. Excitement fills the air! All the kittens are ready for new challenges and ideas. Summer is now a distant memory. "Quiet down!" Marmalade Mike's voice is barely heard over the noise.

School starts with the Pledge of Allegiance at the sound of the bell. The homeroom teacher, Ms. Calista Calico, introduces herself to the class. "Good morning, kittens! I'm from California, and my favorite hobbies are singing and surfing," she tells them. "I'd like each of you to share something about yourself with the class." Everyone has so much to say that there is little time left for the lesson.

Ms. Calico begins, "In our first science lesson, we are going to study evolution. Evolution is how living things change over a long period of time. Does anyone know which came first: the chicken or the egg?"

Camille's paw goes up. "The egg, because dinosaurs came from eggs, and they were around way before chickens."

A tan kitten named Sandra agrees. "Maybe chickens came from dinosaurs! I think that two animals that weren't chickens, like a T. Rex, created a chicken egg and it hatched a chicken."

Their teacher smiles. "Thank you, kittens. Next, we are going to plan a field trip to the Atlanta Zoo. Our focus will be on the many large land animals that live on the African plains. I want you to study the map and practice spelling the names of these animals." Meriwether and Camille sigh. They already know the zoo all too well.

"Is there a zoo in Kalamazoo?" Sprout asks, causing the class to burst into giggles.

"Yes, indeed, Sprout, there is," Ms. Calico replies. "But it's an air zoo. It has old planes, and you can learn how to be a pilot. They even give rides. Who is interested in flying?" Several paws go up. "Maybe your parents will take you to an air museum or the local airport for

Fall Break."

When it is time for recess, all the kittens race to the playground. The hall monitors quickly stop them. "Walk! Don't run!"

Once outside, they take turns climbing trees, swinging on the jungle gym, darting through hoops, digging holes, and splashing in the fountain. After, they enjoy a long drink of water and a fish snack before going inside for their next class.

Math comes easily for all the kittens. They can count birds on a limb, butterflies in a bush, or days until the holidays. Their teacher, Mr. Humperdinck, is impressed with their smarts. "Let's play a game," he says. "We'll take an imaginary trip to the pet store. I'll show you how to estimate the number of fishes in a tank and how to tally the cost of the toys you want to buy." Each time they solve a problem, Mr. Humperdinck gives them a treat. In this way, the class solves a lot of problems. They're ready for harder math!

At the end of the day, the kittens find Marmalade Mike waiting in his yellow bus at the curb. He's working on a crossword puzzle. "Did you have a good first day of school?" he asks.

"Yes, we did!" they meow together. It's quiet on the bus going home as each kitten thinks about the lessons they learned.

In each home that night, parents and big persons feel pride in their kittens as they share stories of their first day of kitty school. They look forward to what the next day will bring.

On the second day of kitty school, Marmalade Mike arrives in the yellow bus right on time at 7:00 a.m. He flashes his red lights to stop oncoming traffic and opens the doors. "How's everybody doing today?" he asks happily. "Are you going to have a purrfect day?"

The kittens think he is silly.

After the pledge, Ms. Calico announces the daily science lesson. "How did the dinosaurs go extinct? You have all read a lot about them. What are some of your ideas of what caused them to disappear?"

All the paws go up. "An asteroid hit the earth and wiped them out," a fluffy gray kitten meows.

"Yes, that's a popular theory," she nods. "There is new thinking that volcanic eruptions around the earth destroyed them. What is most important, however, is that this was the beginning of the Age of Cats. Cats thrived all over the earth. Today, serious scientists suggest that cats were even gods in some civilizations. They were worshipped in the Valley of the Kings in Egypt," she finishes with flair. Her words leave the kittens with much food for thought.

Recess comes, and this time the kittens play at hopscotch, tumbling, stalking, hissing, and growling contests.

The last class of the day is the easiest. They listen to a podcast about meowing. "Oh, we already know how to do that," meow all the kittens.

In a few short weeks, it's time for Fall Break. Some kittens are going to Kalamazoo, some to the Pacific Rim, and others to the Bahamas. Sprout is planning to trek with Adele in Kathmandu. Meriwether and Camille are undecided; they'll probably stay home because Sam expects a visitor from Russia.

10 A Sister for Sprout

Adele is planning a trek in Kathmandu. Since she and Sprout love long, brisk hikes together, she invites him to come along. Sitting at home alone during Fall Break while all his friends are taking cool trips does not sound fun. Nepal, a country so unlike his own, fills him with awe. He can think of nothing more exciting than trekking in Kathmandu!

For several weeks before the trip, Sprout hunts in the library and searches the internet to learn about Nepal. He is especially interested by an article in Kitty Times about Yeti, the creatures like Bigfoot, thought to live in the Himalayas. Do they exist, or are they a myth? Sprout dreams about them on the long flight to Kathmandu.

The head of Yeti Adventures greets Sprout and Adele at the airport. As they drive to their base camp on the mountain, he explains that it will take a day or two to get used to the thin mountain air. They should use the time to prepare for their trek. Jackets, boots, and hats? Check. Backpacks filled with maps, water bottles, flashlights, sunscreen, energy bars, and tuna flakes? Check. Walking sticks for Adele? Check.

Once the trek begins, the guide puts Sprout on his shoulders for a ride atop his backpack. "I am king of the mountain!" Sprout roars.

Despite the setting and his not-so-humble attitude, Sprout thinks about Sandra, the shy, tan kitten he knows at kitty school. He likes the way she rolls over when she sees him on the playground. She lives at Kitty Corner, an animal shelter in Atlanta. Why hadn't she been adopted? Where did she come from? He wonders. "I wish I could have invited her to come with us," he says aloud.

On the second day of the trek, Sprout feels stronger and believes he can climb the mountain forever. Light snow falling on the trail inspires him. "Have you ever seen a Yeti?" he asks the guide.

"Never," he replies. "But I believe they exist."

Adele says she loves her Yeti hat and other Yeti gear but doubts they are real. "At least, I don't expect to see any on this trip," she adds when she sees Sprout frown.

Ahead on the trail, a group of hikers walks toward them. Sprout asks them if they have seen any Yeti. "No, not yet," one says. "But we did see some tracks on the slopes—possibly a snow leopard."

Sprout just can't give up his desire to find a Yeti. He keeps his eyes open for large tracks on the mountain and his ears open for sounds, although he doesn't think Yeti can talk. Sometimes, in a gust of wind, he feels tingly, but that's probably just from being so high up. After all, they are 12,000 feet above the ocean.

On the third day of their stunning trek, the guide points to a herd of yaks. "These animals are vital to us. We depend on them to carry loads, for their rich milk, and for the warmth they provide in our huts in the winter," he says.

They stop in the village below, where the friendly villagers invite them to come in for yak milk tea. Thanking them for the yummy tea, Sprout asks them about Yeti.

"Yes, they live high up in the mountains," a villager answers. "Sometimes, we feel their presence, but we have never seen one," they said.

As they leave the village, Sprout's fur begins to prickle. He can't tell why, but he feels a strange presence nearby. The guide and Adele say they haven't felt anything.

Back on the trail, they see the same shaggy herd of yaks. One of them, wearing a woven blanket, turns slightly. It shows two words clearly woven into the blanket: ADOPT SANDRA!

"What?!" they all exclaim. The guide doesn't understand the message. Adele is confused. Only Sprout knows the meaning of the sign. He tells Adele that Sandra is the name of a sweet kitten at school that lives in the shelter and how much he misses her.

"Can we please visit her when we get back?" Sprout pleads. "I wish we could adopt her so I can have a sister."

For the rest of the trip, they continue their trek along the path often traveled by mountain dwellers and tourists alike. They meet people from all over the world, and they learn to share the trail with yaks carrying sacks of flour, rice, and oranges.

On the seventh day, they return to base camp and then fly home. Fall Break was a big success, and Sprout thanks Adele for such a great trip. However, even before they unpack, he knows there is something they have to do: adopt Sandra!

Together, Sprout and Adele drive to the Kitty Corner shelter. Sandra is so happy to see Sprout that she rolls over seventeen times.

"Why, she's wonderful!" Adele says. "We must adopt her. She will be a perfect sister for you!"

Before leaving the shelter with Sandra in a pink carrier, Adele pauses to ask the manager if she knows where Sandra came from.

"Oh, a stranger dropped her off," she says. "He told

us she was raised by Yetis in Kathmandu. An odd story, don't you think?" Sprout's fur begins to tingle, and once again, he feels that strange presence. He also feels happier than ever because they have adopted Sandra!

11 ONION DOMES

"Fall Break, and we're going nowhere," grumbles Meriwether, thinking about Sprout on his adventure. As he sits on the top railing of the deck, he swishes his tail. He and Camille aren't supposed to be there because of the nine-foot drop to the ground below.

"All we do is watch airplanes fly overhead all day long. I wish we could see one up close. They're so beautiful! If only we could fly in one," Camille says to her brother.

"I've never been in one before either," Meriwether says. The more they think about flying, the more they want to do it.

A few minutes later, Sam comes out onto the deck, jingling his car keys. "What are you doing up there on the railing?" he snaps at the kittens.

"We're watching the airplanes," they answer.

"Well, why don't you come along with me?" he suggests. "I'm going to the airport to meet Boris, our Russian friend from Sochi."

Pearl, who is studying spider webs on the trellis, says, "Go ahead, enjoy the ride. I'll dust and catch crickets in the barn. But when you get back, I'll need your help stringing up the holiday decorations." She's very excited to see Boris, who had adopted her distant relative, Masha, a Siberian Forest cat.

According to Pearl, her great grandfather was a ship's cat out of Seattle, traveling the world. Once, while onshore in the Russian port of Vladivostok, he fell in love with a long-haired Siberian Forest cat. Their five kittens spread out over the vast countryside, wherever luck or fortune took them. Masha's family settled in Sochi, where she was born and where Boris found her. Pearl could not wait to catch up on Masha's news.

Riding to the airport, Meriwether and Camille listen to the story of Masha that Sam tells them, and vow they will one day travel to Russia to meet her.

At the airport, their thoughts quickly shift when they see a sign that says, "Arrivals."

"No running off. Stay in the car," Sam says.

Ignoring Sam's words, they wait only long enough for him to close the door before squeezing through the window he carelessly left open. They tumble onto the sidewalk. Quickly, they scramble past the baggage claim area and bound up the escalator. Sliding past security, they dash around the people at the gate and onto a jet bound for Russia.

Choosing two empty seats, they buckle up and ready themselves for takeoff. As they soar into the sky, Meriwether stares at the stunning views of the clouds and of the Atlantic Ocean far below. He thinks he might want to be a scientist who studies clouds.

Meanwhile, back in the airport, everyone is panicking. When he sees the kittens missing, Sam quickly tells airport security. They begin a full search of the airport. Speakers boom, asking travelers to check their bags. Dogs sniff, hoping to catch their scent. Pictures of the kittens are hung on every wall. But no one can find Camille and Meriwether. The security people promise Sam they won't give up, and they'll let him know as soon as they find them. Still afraid for the kittens, he leaves the airport with Boris. All joy is gone.

Finally, a flight attendant finds Meriwether and Camille in their seats. The news is sent over the radio back to the airport. The air traffic controller tells security, who then call Sam. "The kittens are over the Atlantic Ocean, halfway to Russia. We will have them back tomorrow."

These words do not make Sam feel fully happy. "I can't believe it! These pranks have to stop. No treats for a month!" he states.

Boris smiles at the thought that the kittens are likely on the same plane he had just left.

Several hours later, after a tasty herring dinner, the kittens nap. As the plane lands, Camille wakes up. "Oh," she cries, "look at those beautiful onion domes! Where are we?"

"We're landing in Moscow," Meriwether answers.

The captain comes out of the cockpit to thank everyone for flying with him. "Spasibo! Thank you!" he says.

Meriwether and Camille say, "Spasibo," to the captain.

"Our mother speaks Russian, and she taught us how to say thank you," explains Camille. "Our great, great grandfather fell in love with a Russian cat and moved here. We plan to visit our Russian family while we're here."

"Interesting," says the captain. "But you kittens are stowaways, so you can't leave the plane. You'll go back to Atlanta on the next flight. We liked having you two aboard, but next time you'll need a ticket and your passports."

Meriwether and Camille share a look; they know they will be back.

12 A Loud Crash

Sitting in his favorite chair on the deck, Sam enjoys a morning mug of coffee while looking over the yard. He loves springtime when all the world is waking up. Chipmunks play games of hide-and-seek across the yard, then dart under the fence in a wild-goose chase. His eyes turn to the hummingbird feeder. Two tiny green and gold bodies flitter around each other between sips of nectar.

Pearl sits beside him playing cat's cradle—with one eye on a fat robin.

Crash!

"What was that?" Pearl asks, ears alert.

"Something must have fallen out of the tree," Sam replies, studying the yard.

Branches from the oaks crack and crash to the ground all the time—even in the gentlest breeze. "It must be a limb or those pesky squirrels fighting over an acorn," he mutters as he goes to check it out. Pearl has already bounded across the yard in three giant leaps toward a pile of leaves.

Camille, dizzy and half-buried in the pile of leaves, stirs. She feels the comfort of her mother's tongue licking her face, and she hears her brother nearby.

Camille's sudden drop into the leaf pile brought her a few feet away from where Meriwether sat, watching the birdbath. He, too, heard the crash. Seeing his sister on the ground with her eyes closed, he cries, "Is she dead?"

"Of course I'm not," Camille growls. "I'm fine, and I refuse to go to the vet." Pearl continues licking her daughter's face, glad Camille can speak.

"Where does it hurt?" she asks.

"All over, Mom," Camille admits.

"Can you see?" Meriwether wants to know.

"It's dark!" she replies.

"Open your eyes," her brother commands.

She opens them and looks around. "I see daylight," she answers. "How did I get here, anyway?"

"Don't you remember?" Meriwether asks.

"No. Wait, yes! I was having a cat nap in the hammock, dreaming about summer vacation, when suddenly something swooped down and grabbed me. There were feathers everywhere, and I felt a sharp pain in my back. Then the world went blank."

Seeing the injured cat, Sam knows what to do. In the barn, he finds a cat carrier. Grasping it, he quietly walks to the group. "Camille needs to go to the vet, no matter what she says. Who's coming with me?" he asks.

Pearl's whiskers twitch. "She'll feel better if I hold her paw."

Meriwether pauses. "I would, but I'm in the middle of a bird count." Camille rolls her eyes.

When they get to the vet clinic, the woman at the front desk says, "We can see Camille right away."

After taking several X-rays, the vet asks them to wait for the results. In a few minutes, she returns and pins the X-rays on the wall. "Camille has dislocated her hip," she shows them on the image. "Like most cats when they fall, Camille landed on her feet, but the sudden impact is what caused the dislocation. She also has large scratch marks on her back."

The vet pushes Camille's hip back into place with a sharp pop, then instructs Camille to rest for two weeks. "No tree-climbing and no going down rabbit holes. You can walk, but don't run." She then gives Camille some long-lasting pain medicine and a hug. "You were a good patient, Camille. Get well, and we'll see you in six weeks for your yearly checkup."

"Thank you," Camile says weakly, but the dreadful thought of returning in six weeks causes the normally black and white kitten to turn green.

On the way home, Sam and Pearl wonder about the cause of the crash. As soon as they get out of the car, they settle Camille in her bed on the barn floor so she won't have to climb up to the loft. Then they scour the bushes and trees in the back yard for an explanation.

The answer soon becomes clear: it is not what had caused the accident, but rather who. Perched in the neighbor's pecan tree, a sharp-beaked and feathered creature glares down at them. "Whoo!" it hoots angrily, having been denied its morning breakfast. Luckily for Camille, when the owl rose into the oak tree's highest branches, one of its claws got caught in a twig. It forced the hungry owl to drop the dangling kitten from its claws.

13 Fishing on the Open Sea

"My heavens!" exclaims Sam to Pearl as he trims his beard one warm May morning. "Exactly one year ago, we moved to Atlanta. And the kittens have now finished their first year of kitty school! Let's celebrate and take a trip to Alaska, the Land of the Midnight Sun!"

Meriwether and Camille peer through the screen door, wondering why breakfast is taking so long. They start meowing, which startles Sam and brings him running.

"Oh, there you are! So, it's salmon you want, eh? Ha! Where we're going, you can eat all you can catch!"

A week later, with fishing gear and duffle bags

packed, they've boarded the plane and are ready for takeoff. The kittens fasten their seatbelts and relax next to Pearl and Sam. Smiling at her mother, Camille meows, "Mom, we're so glad you came along!"

Her jewel-green eyes glinted as she replies, "Well, someone has to take charge!"

Later, all eyes swing toward the windows. The earth viewed from above is spectacular: the vast Rocky Mountains, the rugged Pacific coast, icebergs, fjords, deep emerald lakes, endless wilderness. It's beautiful but also daunting, even for the fearless kittens.

As the jet begins its descent to the Anchorage airport, the kittens see Denali—a single mountain standing high above all the other peaks in the snow-capped Alaska range, the highest mountain in North America, Sam tells them.

A short while later, they leave the Anchorage airport in a rented car, turning south around the bay and onto the highway.

As they drive, Sam says, "One summer when I was in college, I took a job on a fishing boat off the coast of

Alaska. I drove there in my old blue car and arrived on the Homer Bluff. The boat I signed up for was called the *Nushagat*. It was equipped with lots of fancy tech that could get weather alerts, test the ocean's depth, find the best fishing grounds, and even see schools of fish.

"Captain Bob Quinn and the fishermen welcomed me aboard. Then we pulled up anchor and chugged into the harbor. Several hours later, the boat slowed, and the fishermen started spinning out the lines. The fumes from the engine, the speed of the lines spinning out, and the chance of getting yanked overboard made my stomach turn," said Sam. "But this was not the time to be seasick, so I paid attention to the crew and began hauling in the catch. It was a good day, and I felt a sense of freedom and pride!"

Rounding a curve, they arrive on the Homer Spit and jump out of the car to stretch their legs, feeling the beauty of summertime in Alaska.

At the harbor, they admire the fleet, and see one boat named Nushagat. "Isn't that the name of your old fishing boat?" Meriwether asks excitedly.

"You're right! " Sam grins. "And we'll be on it to-day!" They walk to the old boat. Captain Bob Quinn steps ashore and greets them. This sea-soaked fisherman had fished all his life; it's clear that seawater runs in his veins. "Ahoy, me hearties! Twenty years has been too long! Welcome back to the Nushagat." This made the kittens giggle.

"He should change the name to the NushaCAT!" Meriwether whispers.

Captain Quinn's weather-beaten eyes stare at the kittens. "It's not unusual to have ships' cats on board, but this is a small ship on dangerous waters. They don't look sea-worthy to me," he said.

"Ahem!" says Sam. "Trust me; these kittens have survived the mighty rapids of the Chattahoochee River; they can handle anything."

"All right," the captain agrees. "They can come aboard as deckhands, but they'll have to stay in the hold and tend the fish. Their job will be to keep them from jumping back into the ocean."

Pearl decided to stay onshore and investigate the

salmon at the canning factory. She watches as the Nushagat heads out to sea. She believed that fair winds will blow her kittens safely back to port.

Below deck, Meriwether and Camille learn all the fish in the hold. "The big flat ones that look like a barn door are halibut, the prickly ones are porcupine fish, the ones with eight arms are octopuses, and ... this is boring," Camille says. "Captain Quinn said we were deckhands, so why can't we be up on the deck?"

Climbing the steps and peering out the hatch, they see gentle waves over a glassy sea and breathe in the salty air. Seagulls following the ship dive for scraps of bait, ignoring the kittens.

At the wheel in the control room, Captain Quinn listens to radio reports and checks the sonar for the ocean's depth, while Sam helps the crew reel out the fishing line behind the boat. The kittens creep toward the stern, where they sit on a coil of rope to observe the fishermen. It's a jolly sight indeed!

But ten minutes later, the kittens are overboard, clinging to a life preserver the crew frantically threw out to them. The kittens can barely see Sam waving wildly in the distance while Captain Quinn rages with a red face.

What went wrong? The coil of rope they had been sitting on was not a rope after all. It was the fishing line. It snatched the kittens as it streamed into the ocean and tossed them into the Gulf of Alaska.

"This is terrible! Here we are, out in the middle of the ocean, bobbing up and down, and no one will come to rescue us," Meriwether cries in between waves.

"Never give up," Camille gasps. "There is always a ray of hope!"

And then a curious dolphin appears beside them, tickling them with its dark nose. It tows them for miles on the life preserver. The kittens don't know where they're going, but at least they're having fun! However, by the end of the afternoon, the dolphin tires of its game and leaves them stranded, far from the Nushagat and from shore.

As the sun sets, their hopes sink. The waves become taller. Camille shivers. "This water is icy! Just how much longer will my fur coat keep me warm?"

Meriwether insists on looking at the bigger picture. "Remember, our great, great grandfather sailed these waters on his way to Vladivostok. We must be somewhere between Alaska and Russia," he guesses.

Camille smiles. "Maybe the friendly dolphin was helping us get closer to land. Are you praying, Meriwether?"

"Yes, that's what shipwrecked sailors do," he replies, his toes nipped by the frigid water. "No stars, no lights, no dolphins. We're just two lonely kittens lost at sea."

14 Out of This World

In the pale twilight, the sad kittens look up and see something glowing. A beam of light cuts through the darkening sky. The static makes their fur stand on end, and it slowly pulls them up out of the swirling sea.

The stream of light warms them from the ocean's frigid waters. Rising higher, they glimpse a glimmering orange orb with blue portholes, one of which now opens for them.

Exhausted from the ocean, Meriwether mews to his sister, "I don't think I can escape this beam!"

Mustering all her strength, Camille replies, "Don't! This is far better than the ocean." As they draw closer to the strange object, Camille says weakly, "Are we entering a blimp?"

"Not this time," replies her stunned brother. "This is a real UFO!"

Feeling lighter than air, they drift inside the UFO. Tiny green figures rush over to stare at them and to touch them with rubbery fingers. The small creatures are about the same size as Meriwether and Camille, but they have six legs, three eyes, and no whiskers. On top of their heads are antennae with knobs that buzz with electricity. Worse, instead of a warm welcome, several creatures march them off to a prison cell on the spaceship.

"We didn't do anything!" the kittens protest, but no one understands them.

They're given a tiny bit of moon-shaped cheese and a milky drink which tastes like mushroom soup. "I'm so hungry, I'll eat anything," Meriwether says, swallowing the strange food. They rest on a cushion that feels more like a bed of nails.

"This beats the ocean, and at least we're together," they agree.

An hour later, a robot unlocks the door and beeps.

"We were swept into the waters of the North Pacific from a fishing boat," Camille tells the robot. "Thank you for rescuing us, but could we please go home—at least to Homer, Alaska?" she says politely. The robot says nothing, but leaves, locking the door behind it.

"We need a plan," Camille says as the cogs in her near-frozen brain begin slowly turning.

Meriwether whispers, "Why don't you sing our story, Camille? You can sing like a nightingale. Maybe you can win them over, and they'll set us free."

Two six-legged guards and the robot come to their prison door and unlock it. The robot delivers a message from the leader of the aliens. "I told him about your request to go to home. The council will decide your fate."

Meriwether and Camille are then led to a meeting room, where the leader and the council wait. The leader of the aliens, who is slightly larger than the other creatures, stares at them with great curiosity. "Do not fear us. We are not unkind, and we don't wish to keep you long. Our only desire is to learn more about life on Earth. We know plants, animals, birds, fish, and insects live there. This is of great interest to us because all creatures are the same on our planet. Please tell us all you know about Earth. After you finish your story, we will release you back into the ocean."

"With all due respect, sir," Camille says, her whiskers trembling, "there's a problem. Our story won't be finished until we get home." Instead of crying, she begins singing in her finest voice.

"Home is where we want to go
with the tall oak trees.
To the great green barn
and the Chattahoochee.
Home to squirrels, wiggly worms
and green-eyed mom.
Home to Sam and our friends,
where all is safe and calm.
Home to Sprout and Sandra,
Whistling Willie, pedaling fast,
Annie, his little brown dog.
Home, home at last!"

"You have touched us with your beautiful voice," says the leader. "We have learned much about life on Earth from your sweet music." he nods to the council. "We believe that Earth is a worthy place to visit one day. For now, I will beam you and your brother back to your mother, who is in the canning factory. We can see that she misses you very much. She is crying as she cans the salmon.

With that, the green alien gives the kittens a jolt of electricity from one of his antennae, sending them away.

When Meriwether and Camille wake up, they see that they're still far from home. The kind-hearted alien had accidentally beamed them to Nome, Alaska! "But Nome is not home," the kittens meow.

The alien leader looks down on Earth and sees his mistake. Lowering his antenna, he quickly sends them to Homer.

Whether a thousand years or one day aboard the UFO had passed, it makes no difference to the kittens. When their eyes blink open, their mother and Sam are hugging them on the pier. It's the biggest cuddle puddle they've ever had! They celebrate so much that several harbor seals swim over to bark and flap their flippers for joy.

"I was filling my one thousand ninety-ninth can of salmon," Pearl says, "When I saw a streak of light in the sky, and suddenly you appeared!"

"Oh, Mom, it's so good to be back on Earth," Camille says. "Thank goodness our adventure is over. Can we go home?"

"Hold on!" says Sam. "Not yet! We haven't seen Denali! The glory of Alaska lies before us." From under his fishing hat, he reminds them that their final chapter in the Great Northwest is to visit Denali National Park. "Hop in the car, my dears, and we're off—it's only two more days. Then we can set our sails for home."

With a spring in their step, the intrepid family climbs into the car, eager to conclude their holiday.

15 Goodbye, Denali

Ahead, rising from the Earth in morning grandness, Denali appears, its peak circled in a halo of clouds. The great mountain is more wonderful than anything the kittens have ever seen before.

Outside the car's windows, Denali National Park is full of wildlife: herds of caribou roam, packs of gray wolves and coyotes run across the tundra, Kodiak bears browse for berries, while golden eagles soar above in lazy circles.

The Denali Park road is closed to cars due to heavy summer traffic. "We can either hike from here or take a bus through the park," Sam says. "The Savage River loop is two miles long, and the bus takes four hours."

"We want to hike," the kittens agree. "We'll be back on the bus for kitty school soon enough."

"Good choice. I'll carry the backpack with our water, treats, and bear spray. We need to stay alert and keep our distance from bears. If we get too close to one, wave your arms and make a lot of noise to frighten it away," he says. "Watch where you walk, too. It's boggy, and we'll probably get our feet wet."

At first, they feel small compared to their surroundings' glory, but soon the creatures of the tundra win them over. Pearl spots a ptarmigan family in the brush, Meriwether surprises a marmot, and Camille sees a flash of red that might be an arctic fox or a red squirrel. Peering through his binoculars, Sam sees two Dall sheep balancing on a cliff.

Beside the rushing water of the Savage River, the family makes their way up the trail. Sam tries calling a moose out of the spruce forest, but none appear. Upstream, halfway through the loop, they see a big black bear standing on a rock in the river. It's a mother showing her two cubs how to fish. They're so cute, splashing in the shallow water along the bank. Pearl smiles while she watches the distracted cubs. "My kittens never pay attention either."

The snow geese feeding in a meadow of cotton grass seem to be honking their goodbye. Is a trumpeter swan high above their heads looking for a lake or calling to them? The sounds of the arctic wilderness fill them with awe. What a nice way to spend their last day in Alaska!

At the visitor center, they buy gifts for their friends, Sprout and Sandra. They also find a picture of a sled dog for Annie.

On the road to Anchorage for their flight home, everyone shares their favorite and least favorite moments of the vacation. Overall, despite the hardships of the trip, they enjoyed their holiday. The high points were the beautiful scenery on land, sea, and air. Going overboard on the Nushagat and being kidnapped by aliens were the lowest points. "Consider these experiences as character-building," Sam says, adjusting the brim of his fishing hat.

From the back seat, Meriwether and Camille tell their stories to Pearl, who is talented enough to write them down. She doesn't miss a single letter, even with the kittens' constant interruptions.

Aboard their flight home, they look out the window one last time. The sun is still peeking over the mountains even though it's late, because during an Alaskan summer the sun never fully sets. Pearl wraps herself around her kittens, and Sam disappears under his fishing hat.

Life settles back to normal after their unforgettable trip to Alaska. The kittens remember the wonders of Denali Park: the untamed country and the animals that roam free. Although their love of water never fades, they prefer rafts and kayaks to fishing boats. Sometimes at night, when they look up into the sky, it seems that the sky winks back.

"Mom, our adventure is over; let's write our book," Meriwether begs his mother. She looks just like a Nile goddess curled up with her kittens on the couch outside the green barn one warm August evening.

Pearl reaches under the cushion and pulls out a small book. "My dears, it's already been done. Chatta-hoochee Cats!"

After reading their story together, the happy cats climb into the loft and begin to purr. The sound of hap-piness can be heard for miles. Sam hears it, too, as he falls asleep.

Acknowledgments

To my publisher, Emily Barrosse, thank you for accepting my manuscript from a sea of children's book submissions. To Sydney Chinowsky, for your joyful editing that created this book for young readers. To Susan Mitchell, for your inspired and beautiful illustrations that breathed life into every chapter. To all others on the Bold Story Press team, for bringing this book to fruition.

To Angus Guberman, Pearl's real-life big person, who dared to fish on a commercial fishing boat in the waters of the Gulf of Alaska, and whose adventurous spirit put power in my pen. He can often be seen rafting on the Chattahoochee with his kids, Gemma and Luke.

To Maxwell Guberman and Olga Postolnikova, for a weekend in the Blue Ridge Mountains, where this book came together above the mists.

To my Sisters, Susannah, and Elizabeth, who never let me quit, and my brother, Jock, for his great generosity in making this book possible.

To Sandra Hughes and the Tuesday afternoon writing class at Gateway Performance Productions.

To Juan Felipe Pérez-Vallejo, for the gift of his laptop now covered in kitten fur.

To Tabby's Place: A Cat Sanctuary, where unlucky cats become lucky.

Bold Story Press is a curated, woman-owned hybrid publishing company with a mission of publishing well-written stories by women. If your book is chosen for publication, our team of expert editors and designers will work with you to publish a professionally edited and designed book. Every woman has a story to tell. If you have written yours and want to explore publishing with Bold Story Press, contact us at https://boldstorypress.com.

BOLD STORY PRESS The Bold Story Press logo, designed by Grace Arsenault, was inspired by the nom de plume, or pen name, a sad necessity at one time for female authors who wanted to publish. The woman's face hidden in the quill is the profile of Virginia Woolf, who, in addition to being an early feminist writer, founded and ran her own publishing company, Hogarth Press.

Made in the USA
Columbia, SC
28 December 2021